SEA SHELLS

Today's malady tomorrow's melody

DR R VISWA KUMAR MD

Contents

Foreword

Sea shells found in sea shore are tiny and are believed to have been Secretly Drifted Ashore. They are Beautiful, Unique and Used to Symbolize Fertlity, Good luck and Fortune.Most Importantly they carry the Sound of ocean Surging through Their Body. The Author who is a Renowed Doctor By Profession, Dwells Deep into Human Psyche by his Keen Observation, Thoughts and Analysis and Comes out with his SHELLS, Aptly termed SEASHELLS. After going through each Mesmerizing Section you can Feel with Certainty Sea Shells may not Contain just Oysters but also PEARLS of Wisdom.Though in a Beach we see Sweep of Sand, Seaweed, Sea Glass and other Incongrous Objects Washed up by the Ocean, it is Sea Shells that Knowingly or Unknowlingly tell us the Great Truth of Life, still lay Undiscovered Before us. This unique book has the same Impact. By reading and listening to all the Sections in the book as a Child listens to the Sea in a Seashell, you become a Word Dreamer Hearing the Murmurs of a World of Dreams. I am completely cofident that you will 'shellbriate' after you finish Reading this Gem of a book

DVNRAJ

A Vibrant Reader.

Prologue

Quotes are quoted as translation of one's own experiences in life. For eons message is passed on from one generation to another by way of sharing their experiences in writing. It is not simple literary work and not about literary skills either. Many times we have to read between the lines.

Unless one dives deep into his heart with deep introspection it is not possible to reflect their experiences in writings like picking pearls in deep sea, hence the title 'sea shells'. Those on shore never know or realise how deep the experience is unless they dwell in their experience. For the same reason quotes do not transform a reader but can only remind to introspect readers' experience.

Failure can teach us more than success in life. Being ignored can teach better than being recognised. Many of us have a false perception of success, happiness and even life in Toto. Until we receive blow due to these false perceptions we lead our life with borrowed ideas of what success, happiness or life is. Nothing is good or bad, everything is an experience. More than the need to learn new things, there is a desperate need to unlearn and undo old and set patterns in our mind creeping into our life. It is the mind which can be your friend or foe, bad master and good servant as well. When we do not identify ourselves in every thought crossing our mind, that is when introspection begins. Witnessing the thoughts is the key that can turn a debacle into a miracle.

I made every effort to reflect my experiences in my own words, avoiding collecting any other quotes to be sure enough not to be influenced by thoughts of other thinkers and also to connect to the reader at its best.

WISDOM

The wisdom of a still mind is greater than the intelligence of the thoughtful mind

Education interferes with wisdom

Our judgmental attitude is not by our wisdom, but due to lack of it as we don't know what we don't know

Wisdom is to realise the complexity of intelligence

The stubbornness of stupidity is greater than the strength of wisdom

when you know the difference between value and price, you have known the difference between wisdom and intelligence

wisdom is to think beyond prejudice

winning an argument may be intelligence, but avoiding it is wisdom

Our judgmental attitude is not by our wisdom,

but due to lack of it as we don't know what we don't know

Plain thinking is possible out of innocence and wisdom, but not out of intelligence

We value anything as per our need, rarely because of our wisdom

Wisdom is to think beyond prejudice

If you know difference between value and price, you have known difference between wisdom and intelligence

Knowledge is to know what is.. wisdom is to know what is not..

The paradox is ignorance is not knowing, wisdom is knowing that you don't know,

in between intelligence alone troubles

Being kind is the zenith of wisdom

Wisdom is better than skill

skill is better than knowledge

knowledge is better than information

information is better than ignorance

ignorance is better than arrogance

FREEDOM

Freedom arises in mind, never from circumstances

Freedom is naturally inherent, we are trying to
snatch away man-made shackles

Growing beyond wants is freedom, beyond needs is
nirvana

Freedom doesn't come by defining territories,

it comes by not defining territories at all

Freedom can't be purchased,

it is to be earned by the realisation

Freedom is the highest form of luxury that even the
rich can't afford

Seek not opinion, freedom begins...

opine not, peace begins

Rights are ignored when freedom is deprived,

Responsibilities are ignored when freedom is abused

Freedom is to think speak and act the same

Freedom is your degree of belief in it

INTELLIGENCE

It's not intelligence, but adaptation that helps in growth

Intelligence tries to analyse while innocence enjoys things as they are

Intelligence doesn't allow you to perceive its limitations

Intelligence when matures becomes wisdom

Intelligence lets you take pride in knowledge
wisdom humbles you making you realise ignorance

Intelligence by itself can be asset or liability

Love

Love is the purest of all fine feelings. Lust is that of mind while love is that of the heart(not physical). Until lust matures into love, lust keeps bothering for physical or sexual gratification.

LOVE

Love is the highest form of respect,
trust is the highest form of love

Love confers peace
peace finds love

Lust is the quality of mind
Love is the quality of Heart

Loving is giving always

PEACE

only those who know internal peace can give it to
others

Expectations bring agitation, hope confers peace

Peace within you shows peace around

striking a balance between polarities of mind
..ensures peace of mind

peace emerges from acceptance, acceptance comes
from understanding ,understanding is made possible
by open mind

Heart with no faith is accompanied by mind with no
peace

Nothing or no one is worth costing our peace

when you see good in others, if not anything ...at
least it keeps you in peace

Peace is difference between needs and wants

Mind with no conflicts rejoices in peace

Complying confers peace instead of complaining

Peace conferred by trust

ACCEPTANCE

Acceptance is optimism, compromise is pessimism

Perfection is an illusion, acceptance is resolution

stress is the difference between acceptance and unacceptance

acceptance comes from understanding
Understanding comes from an open mind

Seeing things as they are is acceptance

Understanding allows acceptance

Acceptance of limitations allows you to grow beyond them

Do not accept the definition of success given by society

Impatience and unacceptance take their pound of
flesh in life

22

RESPONSIBILITY

selfishness reminds only your rights.., selfless thinking alone reminds your responsibilities

Responsibilities entitle rights

Respect is one's right and others responsibility too

Any fool can desire but wise focus to deserve

Wish is a dream, ambition is a vision

For a viable relationship think of your responsibility and others rights

not your rights and others responsibility

No one has rights over other

but we are responsible for how we treat others

HOPE

Expectations might disappoint, but hope never does

Morning is the dawning of another opportunity at
the horizon of hope

Hope beyond hope, gives a long rope

Hope is the bridge between flourishing and
perishing

Hope is better than reasoning because we don't
know what we don't know

Problems at times may be inevitable, but to worry or
not is our choice

Hope infuses life to life

Hope and enthusiasm are two wheels of life

when hope is nurtured , we nourish the future

There's no dearth of opportunities when there's
hope

Hope in simple terms is 'allowing unknown
possibilities'

Hope beyond hope

Being hopeful against all odds is pragmatic,
not dogmatic

Hope is the mother of patience

Hope is work oriented, expectation is result oriented

Fortune favours those who nurture hope

The biggest handicap in life is a lack of hope or
confidence,
there are no other limitations in life

Expectations bring agitation, hope confers peace

When hope remains everything else will remain

Hope against all odds is allowing possibilities
unknown to us

The principle of the benefit of doubt rests on the
hope

Gratitude

Gratitude is among the noblest virtues one can have and reverence for what we possess or are blessed with. In a way, to be grateful is to be happy.

GRATITUDE

if not anything gratitude reduces stress as it
antagonises greed

Do not pray only when you fall prey be ever grateful

More selfish you are, more anxious you will be

when we ignore what we are blessed with, we will
be ignored to be blessed

Gratitude is the best remedy for greed

The most precious ornament is a smile, richest by
wealth is gratitude

Price for lack of gratitude is 'not being happy'

The advantage of the attitude of gratitude is ...it lets
you realise the value of things,

before you lose them...

Possessiveness

Possessiveness is not a noble virtue as believed. It is a sort of insecure feeling attached to a person or a thing. The only one who is confident that what he deserves will be his will never be possessive.

CONTENTMENT

Contentment is not containment

Less possessive you are more you will possess

Contentment is wisdom to be happy with what you
have

Anything in excess is poison

Mental comfort is greater than physical luxury

You are not healthy if you are not happy
You are not wealthy if you are not content

Contentment is not compromise
It's an ability to be happy with what you are

WORD

words are empty, actions speak for themselves

The tone of speech conveys more than words

when you are sure enough , explanations are never lengthy

If words could convey what we mean,

There would be no arguments

Communication is the toughest task despite our ability to talk

Words are for communication, eyes are for expression

Words do not contain meaning.., they actually contain meaning

Words do not convey meaning until there's right
perception...

Meaning may be same bout perceptions are not

Anger

Anger is predominantly shown in a helpless state. Those reactive, show anger while those who are proactive have the right approach for resolving the issues

SILENCE

People who do not understand your silence will
never understand your words too

Less you know more you speak

more you know less you speak

when silence prevails you have realised the ultimate
truth that you know nothing

The more you understand the futility of words more
silent you become

As is the sky for stars so is the silence for words

Those who are intimate need no words for
communication

for those who are not no word can communicate

ETERNAL LIFE

Meditation is a shift from mindless thoughts to
thoughtless mind

All meanings lose their meanings on reaching
absolute

Higher the plane of thinking more universal our line
of thinking becomes

A drop merging in ocean,

becoming an ocean is devotion

Living in a moment is different from living for a
moment

One has to blossom on their own

On reaching absolute all meanings lose their
meanings

Being ritualistic is in contrast to being spiritualistic

Meditation settles all the agitation

Meditation is technically bringing the subconscious mind more and more to the conscious level

Meditation is a way of deconditioning and unlearning

Meditation magnetises the mind attracting orderliness

Meditation is not controlling the mind its neither concentrating mind it is merely allowing thoughts to settle like ripples of water in a lake

Meditation makes you shed what you are not leading to self-actualization

Meditation transforms ritualistic to spiritualistic

Meditation is essentially a way of unlearning what all we learned and stored in our subconscious mind for aeons

Progeny is an indirect expression of instinct for
immortality

When your body speaks you are animal

When your mind speaks you are a man

When your soul speaks you are god

Life evolves from selfishness to selflessness

Selfishness is to ensure existence

Selflessness is to live in eternity in oneness

Expecting a change in circumstances is like
expecting road traffic to change for your comfort
ride

Joy

Joy is a higher state than being happy and one can be joyful unconditionally like a kid, an artist involved in the performance. Likewise when we do things just for the joy of it with no expectations.

JOY

Perpetual thinking is a sheer search for joy until you
find it within

Joy isn't in physical comforts but in mental comfort

Greater the challenge, sweeter the success

There are not merely seven wonders in world,
if you care enough to see everything is a wonder

When in cloud nine everything looks fine

Seasons and reasons can not bring lasting joy, but
your attitude can

Be playful as there is no replay

The joy of journey in itself is destiny

Sainthood is evolving to childhood

The joy of life is at the doorstep, it's our ignorance
that doesn't let us open the doors

Comfort comes from luxury, joy comes out of
nothing

Do not look for joy in life, Look for life in joy

Taste the joy of being engrossed in what you do,it
makes the job effective and effortless

The more you define life, the less you fit into
it...enjoy being not becoming

it's not what you carry but how you carry is the
burden or joy

it's not a festival that brings joy, but it's the joy that
makes any day festive

The joy of giving is the antidote for greed

The joy of life is the sum of the joy of small things in
life

Nothing is good enough until we start enjoying small
things in life

Lamenting on what you don't have,

doesn't let you enjoy what you have

Those who do not enjoy the journey,

can not enjoy destination too

.life is all about journey not destiny

Giving is joy, expecting is agony

Given the choice between entertainers and well-
wishers,

We prefer spending with entertainers because we
fail to find joy with ourselves

intelligence tries to analyse while innocence enjoys
simply what is

Contents of mind don't keep you content

Emptying the mind is filling the heart with joy

There is nothing that is not enjoyable right from
sunrise to sunset

42

Seriousness is always borrowed

We often mistake seriousness for sincerity

Joy begets joy, melancholy begets melancholy

See to watch

Hear to listen

Touch to feel

Talk to express

Think to feel

As life is all about living the moment

Happiness

We are happy conditionally only when something happens as per our expectations

HAPPINESS

Being happy is a choice open to everyone

if you can't be happy with what you have,
you can never be happy be whatever you have

I'm not healthy if I'm not happy and not wealthy if
not content with what I have

Human needs are beyond physical level.,
That's why we aren't happy even after meeting all
our physical needs

Difference between needs and wants is like
difference between cost and price

There are many around who can make you unhappy,
there's hardly anybody who can keep you happy
except yourself

Achieving all that you want may not be in our hands
entirely, but being happy with what you have is in
our hands

Excitement is a wave, happiness is a flowing river

Solitudes is bliss while loneliness is a curse

Mind merits to make the life merrier

There's no 'way to happiness, happiness is the way

We blossom; when we see the brighter side of the day

Happiness is a choice we can choose, doesn't come with fortunes

We go on trying to invent happiness, but it's always a discovery

The best ornament that anyone can afford is a smile, luxury that even money can't buy us is happiness

Do not mistake excitement for happiness, excitement is short-lived while happiness is long-lasting

Success gives excitement,

fulfillment gives happiness

Happiness is not a purchasable commodity,

it's an attitude, being happy

Planning to be happy is the biggest hurdle for
happiness,

being happy is the way

Until you are yourself nothing ever gives you
permanent happiness

Health and happiness are natural qualities of body
and mind,

we made them commodities to purchase

Happiness is not by doing but by being

Those who value pleasures alone can't value
happiness

When you unlearn to be unhappy what remains is
happiness

Happiness comes out of only gratitude

The joy of giving doesn't let you borrow happiness
from others

Learning to be happier is making life easier

don't wait for life to get easier to be happier

If you are not happy with yourself it is loneliness

if you are then it is solitude

The worth of your life is not how successful you are,
but how happy you are

No one can teach others how to be happy

Life is a quest for happiness, we try to reach the
moon and stars till we find it in ourselves

Nothing like being happy with yourself

Life is a journey from what we seek to what we need

Realizing what really confers happiness

Ego

Ego is an exaggerated projection of selfishness for identity. It goes far beyond self-respect or self-esteem and even at the cost of respect for others.

EGO

Ego is like alcohol, temporarily pleasurable,

thereafter its hangover can cost anything in life

where vanity prevails sanity vanishes

Ego isolates, equanimity unites

We do not understand until we need to...

The way we treat ourselves is the way world treats
us

Wider you think, larger the world you belong to

Trust worthiness is possible only in a relation with
no motives

Be playful as there's no replay

winner of the argument is loser

Paying attention is soothing, but seeking attention is
painful

More you indulge in identity crisis,

more you lose your identity

Less you react more control you have over you

Arguments instigate for more complaints that never
occurred before

Feeding ego is starving for togetherness

Ego is a sign of insecurity, equanimity is a sign of
self-esteem

criticism satisfies your ego when you yourself don't
have an identity

when you judge people bridge for communication
gap vanishes

self-pity is an escape from introspection, ego is
beyond introspection, self-esteem is the result of
introspection

As much as you dwell in past,

so much so you forego the future

When ego drives, relation takes back seat

Love alone is an antidote for ego and selfishness

Fear of losing respect is ego

Misunderstanding is a liability for one who
misunderstands

not for one who is misunderstood

Civilization should teach bridging the gaps, not
building the walls

Reasons are cosmetics for our hypocrisy

Self-esteem

This is an expression of self-respect striking a balance between self-pity and ego. One who believes in self-respect neither stoops down for his gains nor insults others for his wants.

SELF ESTEEM

Lamenting on past breeds self-pity, living in the present builds self-esteem

Seeking attention doesn't let you be' yourself

Being different is different from being wrong

The present is the best present, presented to us each moment, make the best of it

Self-pity is an escape from introspection, ego is beyond introspection, self-esteem is the result of introspection

I am what I am when I do not try to impress others impressing others is imprisoning yourself

A thin line between ego and self-esteem is respect for others

Self-esteem neither allows to insult others nor it
allows others to insult you

Being ignored teaches a better lesson than being
recognized

Procrastination

Procrastination is merely comforting your mind for not doing the job today, but it is never a decision to do it tomorrow.

TIME

colossal waste of time in our life is by 'dwelling in thoughts' that serve no purpose

Today makes your tomorrow

Each day unravels unknown possibilities

Past glory is immaterial today...
Today makes your tomorrow

Never take delay as denial

Sometimes problems are not be solved,
but they are to be dissolved in time

Time invested is life invested, be it on anything

Time spent in complaining is the time wasted
in life

If you remember your own responsibilities,

you won't have time to blame others

57

Being a busy bee, finding time for yourself is the
nectar you are fluttering for

Belief

Belief is always a borrowed opinion or idea. We believe just because we choose to believe irrespective of facts or truth. Believing a person, or an idea, or religion is all just the matter of our choice we made to believe in.

BELIEF

Believe not all that you think

Belief is borrowed, truth is realised

Sense or nonsense, it's all about how we bother to understand

Looking for what you learned is a fact, learning from what you look at is truth

Religious and geographical boundaries are arbitrary, imaginary, and illusory

Heart believes in magic, the mind asks for logic

our beliefs are our stumbling blocks

We choose belief over truth because we are comfortable with the belief

our beliefs decide our choices, while facts decide consequences

Belief is what you choose to believe, fact is what you
are supposed to believe in

Freedom is your degree of belief in it

The more you believe in your freedom more you feel
free

Seeing isn't believing when we have our own view

Self-pity

Self-pity is a sort of escapism to face the truth and makes us ignore our responsibility or contribution to our condition. A sort of pleasure we derive by feeling sorry for ourselves.

ATTITUDE

No one can teach us how to be happy, it's an attitude

Repenting is welcoming while self-denial is to be denied

You are sum of your choices

The difference between needs and wants is like the difference between cost and price

Hoping is waiting without questioning, Expecting is questioning without waiting..

Whatever you are not changing you are choosing

Being different is different from being wrong

Helping hands do not look for reasons

Mistakes are better than No takes

Success and failure definitions in childhood nips
their natural growth in bud

Every day is a gift but gift isn't in the box,

Its in the way you unbox

You are as happy as you are willing to be...

There will be sea of change if you change the way
you see

Outer world is reflection of inner world

its not the skill but will that matters

Any fool can desire, but wise focuses to deserve

Failure is reward for those focusing on obstacles,
while success is for those focusing on target

so long we feel that we are right always, no
communication or understanding is possible

insecurity is root of selfishness

No one ever changes unless there are compelling
conditions

Let us go with let go attitude

Gratitude is the ultimate attitude

Being genuinely interested brings the best in what
we do

There is no substitute for goodness

Let us be what we can be

How you talk matters more than what you talk

Being cautious is different from being anxious

Hankering over results spoils the effort

In every way in everything overdoing is
counterproductive

One can live without wealth or education but not
without the right attitude towards life

Taking something for granted may cost you
something you can not afford later

How we view matters more than what we see

Taking for granted is unbecoming of anybody of
anything

The beauty of a flower doesn't determine its
fragrance

Everything follows attitude with certitude

The altitude of success is determined by attitude

A bad attitude is truly a disability

Our judgmental attitude is not by our
wisdom,

but due to lack of it as we don't know what we don't
know

The advantage of the attitude of gratitude is ...it lets you realize the value of things,

before you lose them...

Age cannot cage you when you have the right attitude

The problem of a problem lies in our attitude towards the problem

Where knowledge can not win attitude can

Regret is acting without thinking

Repentance is thinking without acting

Being opportunistic deprives you of further opportunities

Ingratitude

Ingratitude is almost ubiquitous in our lives and this world. Opportunistic people tend to show ingratitude and generally feel their needs are their only priority. In a way projection of selfishness, but it's a liability all through, that can never confer lasting happiness.

VALUE

Everyone knows the price, not many can know the value

Living together doesn't make a home, but togetherness does

Patience is a sign of dedication

Availability or unavailability is the sole reason why we value or not something

Prices can be displayed.

But its value can't be…

Depends on how much you value

when you know the difference between value and price,you have known the difference between wisdom and intelligence

We value anything as per our need, rarely because of our wisdom

Everything is all about importance you attach to it

Those who value pleasures alone can't value
happiness

So long warmth of the sun

Fragrance of flowers

Mellow of breeze

Are not allowed how does it matter even if it is a
mansion

Envy

Envy is a sign of weakness. It's the play of mind for mental comfort by not acknowledging the success of others. One who is only focused on the job at hand has neither time nor attention for what is being done by others.

PROBLEM

Every problem is disguised form of its own solution

When you don't have the proper vision you don't see
solutions for problems within your sight

Every problem is teaching us to grow beyond our
limitations

impatience makes you suffer from what you do not
want to suffer from

Every problem is disguised form of its own solution

Avoiding a problem takes you close to problem
indeed

Problems are 'the way we learn to grow beyond our
limitations

More you blame others for your problems,

less inclined you are to solve them

Overthinking is self-generating a problem,

and then wishing it never happens

72

Problems at times may be inevitable, but to worry or
not is our choice

Sometimes problems are not be solved,

but they are to be dissolved

SIMPLICITY

Take pride in the simplicity

The greatest realisation is to know that the simplest
things aren't as simple as they seem

The best way to learn is by teaching,

And best way to teach is being an example

Mind is the seat of complexity while the heart is the
seat of simplicity

simplicity glorifies the personality

Simplicity is simply recognizing unwanted

Life isn't simple until you realise its simplicity

Cynic

Being cynical is conditioned thinking we are used to. Despite all blessings a cynic keeps complaining about anything and everything. They are generally found mistaking their ignorance for knowledge trying to judge all they come across.

MIND

None can trouble you as much as your own mind

More you resist thought more it troubles ,
more you accept more it surrenders

Past is memorised
Future is imagined
Present is felt

Believe not all that you think

Less you react more you have control

Failure is reward for those focusing on obstacles,
while success is for those focusing on target

I'm what I'm when I stop trying to impress people

Being opportunistic,

deprives further opportunities

interdependency is welcoming , but not merely dependency

Less you think more you feel the present

Anxiety is misuse of imagination

Being cautious Is different from being anxious

As you think so you see

Mistaking our thoughts as feelings leads to unwanted emotions

Wisdom dawns in open mind and obscured in biassed mind

Thinking is an ability,it shouldn't disable us

Diversity should teach us to grow beyond our prejudices

It's the mind that makes moments, not events

Instinct is greater than intelligence

Your vision makes your world

Open eyes with an open mind

Redundancy of mind makes us ignore the abundance
of life

Ideas have destiny while thoughts do not have

Our will is magic lamp that can bring all that you
wish for

Men are arithmetic, women are enigmatic

It's what you do that decides not what you think

It's not eyes that let you see the world, but mind

Postponement is merely freeing your mind from the
guilt of not doing your job today,

but never it is a decision to do it tomorrow

Wider you think larger the world you belong to

Sex is the language of the body

A relation is the language of the mind

Union is the language of the soul

Being unbiased is the agility of the mind, being
biassed is its fragility

complaining is the conditioning of the mind, not due
to conditions of life

Bloomy or gloomy.... All in the mind

As you think so you see

The beauty of thought is the beauty of life

Mind with no preconceived ideas has ever-
expanding horizon of thinking

Being healthy and being happy are natural qualities
of body and mind

What mind doesn't know eyes can't see

Life is as complex as the mind

Reprogramming of mind is nothing but being aware
and conscious about what we think and what we do

Being healthy and being happy are natural qualities
of body and mind
But we made them purchasable commodities

None can trouble you as much as your own mind

As is the mind so is the day ahead

Doubting mind selectively focuses on negative
thinking

Bloomy or gloomy, all in the mind

Perception of life is a reflection of your own mind

None can deceive us more than our own mind

Mind the merits to make life merrier

The complaining mind makes life a hell

: mind by itself can horrify or glorify any experience

Mind with no conflicts is life with no disputes

A balanced mind acts, mind with polarities react

when you do not mind,
it doesn't matter whatsoever

Eyes and ears are not open unless you are open-
minded

Life is simple, but the mind is complex

None can fool you or Harm you as much as your own
mind

your thoughts influence present, determine future,
can't undo past...be mindful of that

The positive aspect of negative thinking is,

it's a checklist reminding possible hurdles to
overcome

One effective means to de stress to remain open-
minded

More the options, the more the conflicts in mind.

choicelessness is bliss

Mind is to think,

not to carry impressions

The mind has no boundaries

Mind that's free from conflicts keeps the heart
blossoming

Seeing is believing-doubting mind says you see what
you believe faithful heart says

Wisdom of a still mind is greater than the
intelligence of the thoughtful mind

Freedom arises in mind, never from circumstances

Lust is the quality of mind

Love is the quality of Heart

striking a balance between polarities of mind
..ensures peace of mind

peace emerges from the acceptance,

acceptance comes from understanding,

understanding is made possible by an open mind

Heart with no faith is accompanied by the mind with
no peace

Mind with no conflicts rejoices in peace

Understanding comes from an open mind

selfishness reminds only your rights, selfless
thinking alone reminds your responsibilities

Meditation is a shift from mindless thoughts to
thoughtless mind

Meditation is technically bringing the subconscious
mind more and more to the conscious level

Contents of mind don't keep you content

Emptying the mind is filling the heart with joy

Health and happiness are natural qualities of body
and mind,

we made them commodities to purchase

Poised mind emerges from nonduality

An open mind opens all possibilities,

while conditioned mind curtails possibilities

Regret is acting without thinking while repentance
is thinking without acting

Conquering one's own mind is conquering all the
evil

When thought, word, and deed are coaxial mind
remains still

Simpler the thinking simpler the life and happier it
is

Roses are not without thorns, what you look at
makes all the difference

84

Prejudice

Prejudice is an extended belief. Prejudice and belief as it sounds need not be judicious. This prejudice can be seen from an individual level to a communal level.

OPINION

let's guard ourselves against our own opinions as
they aren't facts always

Do not judge, opine or conclude... just be aware of
facts

Opinions are clouds obscuring the shine of truth

Likes and dislikes can't be reasoned out

Rushing to conclusions is aborting further
possibilities

Opinions are not necessarily facts

All our thoughts emanate from our opinions, much
of our opinions are our own perspectives

Drop opinions, much of stress will be gone

Seek not opinion, freedom begins...

opine not, peace begins

87

Our tendency to opine is like flow of water along the slope

It can not change its direction on its own, unless we check

KNOWLEDGE

Mistaking our ignorance for knowledge is the most vulnerable state

The joy of innocence is greater than the pride of knowledge

Allowing is enough for light to dispel the dark

Defrost your impressions in the light of truth

Knowledge isn't knowledge but its information within known confines

Education isn't about knowledge, its about wisdom

The difference between literate and illiterate is,

illiterate will have common sense while literate loses even that

We are what we seek

So long literacy is mistaken for education.., it can
never be educative

Realising my ignorance helped me more than my so-
called knowledge

Philosophy isn't heights of knowledge,

but it's the art of unlearning realising our ignorance

Knowledge is to know what is.. wisdom is to know
what is not.

Memory is mistaken for knowledge

Literacy is mistaken for education

LIFE

Wonderment is the elixir of life

Take time to live, life has so much to give

Utility of money we all know pretty well but to
realise its futility,

it takes lifetime

Each of us contributes to life around us, be it good or
bad

Riches do not bring richness to life

Make the world your home, not the home your world

Discipline isn't a pattern of life but its sign of
commitment

Naturally aligned life inherently nurtures
immortality

Life isn't made of years but made of moments

Life is all about aesthetics, not economics

Life isn't all about riches but is about abundance

Being too selfish can make your world too small to
live in

Being sincere doesn't necessarily mean being
serious,

fun can't be missed in life

life is the journey from what we seek to what we
need

Returns are proportionate to what you invest, no
discounts in life

You can not own your possessions and can not
disown your virtues

To savour the flavour of life, mind that journey in
itself is destiny

Life is mechanical only because we take things for granted

what it takes for living is the cost of living, how we want to live is the price we pay for it

Nothing is good enough until you start appreciating small things in life

Lessons of failure are more contributory to life than rewards of success

The more you define life, less you fit into that

Simpler the thinking happier the life

The more you complain, more painful the life is , more grateful you are happier it is

Living in present is a renewal of life afresh each moment, disconnecting past

Life is made of moments, not years

It is not the span of life but, depth of life matters

Life perishes not in poverty but in pessimism,
flourishes not with riches but with optimism

Life is more miserable when you don't take
responsibility for what you are, Blame a million, life
doesn't get better

Life is always how you take it,

not how it is

Much of life is consumed in planning to live, rather
than living

The worth of life isn't how successful you are, but
how happy you are

Count the merits in life that make it merrier

Life is too short to waste on complaints

Life isn't about what you have, it's all about what
you are

The only way to realise worthier things in life is by
realising things that are worthless...never before
that...

Wider the perspective of life,

Wider the spread of mental energy

Living life full means loving life for what it is

Do not look for joy in life, Look for life in joy

Deeper the roots taller we grow

colossal waste of time in our life is by 'dwelling in
thoughts' that serves no purpose

Time invested is life invested, be it on anything

Time spent complaining is the time wasted in life

Life isn't simple until you realise its simplicity

Life is as complex as the mind

Perception of life is a reflection of your own mind

The complaining mind makes life a hell, not
complaining itself makes life much better

Mind with no conflicts is life with no disputes

It's not the achievement but amusement that makes
life lively

The abundance of life lies in enjoying simple things

How you want to live is the price you pay for it

Materialism teaches tact of living
Spiritualism teaches the art of living

Life isn't simple until you realise its simplicity
Realisation isn't simple unless you struggle more
than you need top

Life has no purpose, life by itself is its purpose

Faith

Faith here I do not refer to religious faith. Faith is such a perception of mind which is unquestionable, as the faith of children in parents, a student's faith in his teacher, faithful partner. The spiritual journey is all about faith in eternal truth.

FAITH

Faith is beyond logic that can do all the magic

The brightness of day is the same for all; but brighter for those who open their eyes wider

Spiritualism is not against materialism but it is rather its extension

Faith makes probability a possibility

Belief is blind while faith is foreseeing

Do what you have to do until you can do what you want to do

'Seeing is believing'….' the doubting mind says,…

'You see what you believe'…Faithful heart says

where there's faith there is patience

It's not the ability that brings faith but it's faith that
brings the ability

Faith is a perception, doesn't ask for proof

Where there is no faith, there is anxiety

Faith alone relieves insecurity

Heart with no faith is accompanied by the mind with
no peace

Faith is not against logic, it's beyond

Dependency

Dependency is the deadliest of all, particularly psychological dependency. Financial and physical dependency may be momentary. But when it comes to psychological dependency, unless one makes an effort it is hard to break the shell. Overprotected children are more likely to suffer from this even in their adulthood. The priceless blessing a child can have from parents is to learn life skills when parents allow their children to face on their own what they are confronted with and can rise to occasion when in need.

Trust

Belief, trust, faith all seem to mean more or less the same. But belief can dogmatic, trust is something about the trustworthiness of a person or an idea or a concept. Trust is based on some prior experience to realise trustworthiness. Faith is beyond belief, trust, and something that never asks for proof even because it is beyond all this. Faith in truth is the best example

CARE

Self-respect and self-confidence go together, one takes care of other

Take a break before you break

You will only understand when you care enough

More watering doesn't hasten to flower, just allow it to blossom

A cocoon is a safe haven, but unless it's broken open butterfly can't find its world

The true parents are those who give social birth to their children but not a physical birth

Fencing is to protect, not to prevent the growth

Care enough to becared enough

It's Not what you give your friends or family

but what you made them feel lasts longer

102

caring is the only sign of concern

Daydreamer

Daydreamer keeps dreaming and never believes in his dreams coming true, but simply enjoys dreaming. This is a virtue of lazy people, in general, hoping for a miracle to happen to change their lives

FATE

Believing in fate is an excuse to give up

Predestination is a preconceived notion, what you
are today decides what you will be tomorrow

Fate keeps changing incessantly

Vulnerability is by the degree of belief in it

When you do not believe it does not exist

We are not born to suffer from past karma
But only to be more humane in the future ahead

Astrology accounts for probability, but not for
predictability

Today is the tomorrow you worried about yesterday

Destiny is something you create by your thought,
word, and deed

Not something that is predetermined

Past glory is immaterial however glorious it might
be

As what you are today decides what you will be
tomorrow

RESPECT

Respect is one's right and others responsibility too

Harmony in life emerges from mutual respect

Toughest is to understand, easiest is to blame

Patriotism is not just saluting the flag, but being a responsible citizen

Respect earned by virtues is never lost

Intimacy is not a licence to disrespect

Respect is an indispensable element in any relation

Everyone has the right to be respected and the responsibility to respect

Love is the highest form of respect,
trust is the highest form of love

Fear of losing respect is ego

Self-respect and self-confidence go together, one takes care of other

Respecting fellow humans is the only sign of a cultured man

EXPERIENCE

Emotions are the price you pay for the reward of experience from past

Imperfection is the impetus for perfection

Grow through what you go through

Every malady is a futures melody like a bamboo turns into a flute

There is no substitute for experience

Its never before a bee flutters for miles it finds its honey

Good judgment comes from bad experience, experience comes from a bad judgment

Mind is a reflection of your experience, while again experience is a reflection of your mind

: mind by itself can horrify or glorify any experience

Experience can not be taught

Adversity is the best university

FRIEND

See a friend in everyone, communication gets
easier....

because that's when we talk with no motive

A friend is the best resort

Nothing matters in friendship except friendship

Friends are those with whom you can be yourself

Not a friend in need
A friend is all that I need
friendship is not a deed

Any nonsense can make sense with a friend...
treasure them

You are not what you are not
When you are With a friend

If there is any relation in life with no motives that is only friendship

The best part of friendship is we can choose them in life

UNDERSTANDING

You don't owe an explanation for those who
understand

No explanation will suffice for those who do not
understand

You can not make people understand you unless
they are willing to

The toughest job in daily life is to communicate and
to understand

The reasoning of a reason is reasonable for those
who understand

understanding requires

willingness and open mind

Briefer the explanation greater the understanding

until it is obligatory we never bother to understand

we are more curious to understand things around

But not curious enough to understand people around

understanding and reasoning of our every thought

is what self realisation is

when you know yourself, you will know every one

when you understand truth facts are better understood,

when you can afford to ignore, idea to understand never occurs

misunderstanding is liability for one who misunderstands

not for one who is misunderstood

even when we are wrong we want others to understand

but even when others are right we are not inclined to understand

RELAXATION

Doing nothing once in a while is the important thing
on our 'to-do list

Relaxation is the best remuneration

Work is worship, while relaxation is boon

fulfilling responsibilities can make you relax better
than when you claim your rights and privileges

truth sets you free and keep you relaxed however
harsh it may be

SUCCESS

envying someone's success, no way makes your life
better

Success is relative

At times losing is winning without our knowledge

If you can't be happy even after succeeding in all
that you worked for

You are not successful

Do not accept the definition of success given by
others

If success can't make you a better person then it is
failure

Success shouldn't reach your head

Failure shouldn't reach your heart

Success in anticipation of appreciation is not the one
meant for you

116

Let the success speak for itself, be an underdog

COMPARISON

Being better than someone might need a comparison

But being best doesn't need

Let us learn to coexist and cooperate than to compete or compare

Comparing yourself with others is the gravest insult you are inflicting on yourself

We are not here to prove ourselves to anybody

But to be yourself

comparison is the worst ever insult

self esteem doesn't let you compare yourself with others

EDUCATION

I'm responsible for what I speak,

but not what you understand

Rethinking is better than regretting

Understanding is far beyond judging, not many can reach

Judge a man by his questions rather than his answers...Voltaire

Invoking interest to learn is the best thing teacher can do to pupil

The real measure of our wealth is how much we would be worth if we lost all our money

if it doesn't challenge you,

it doesn't change you

Growing is not ageing but becoming wiser

So called education interferes with wisdom

If it doesn't make you think it is not education

Memory is mistaken for knowledge
literacy is mistaken for education

The difference between an illiterate and a literate is
illiterate retains common sense while literare loses
even that

Hazard of education is false sense of perception of
knowledge

Best way to teach is by being an example
and best way to learn is by teaching

TRUTH

Truth alone gives courage to speak or listen

religious and geographical boundaries are arbitrary,
imaginary and illusory

Trying to be normal is different from being natural..
You don't know what nature manifests through you

Truth is absolute

Realised souls do not speak of their experience
because truth has no attributes to describe

When it is truth, you don't have to memorise

When everything else vanish what remains is truth

Truth is absolute, eternal and universal

One who realises truth doesn't belong to any
religion

Every religion belongs to him

CONCLUDING LINES

Every problem we are confronted with, all has begun in mind. Any remedial measure at physical level is not bringing about a lasting solution.

A poor fellow even after earning enough for his needs and even beyond to the extent of amassing wealth, still runs after money. A criminal even after being punished for his crime once he is out of prison he continues to commit crime. An illiterate even after being imparted education is only becoming an educated fool, but not wise. War can never offer a solution to any dispute permanently because disputes among the nations and boundaries are perpetual and not just about any one given issue. To put it simply, an army or defense is never an answer for peace. It is as ridiculous as having sex for protecting virginity.

Every problem plaguing the world has started only in mind and can only come to end in mind and not by any physical measures or methods. It is not about wealth or education or scientific advancement we need to worry about from individual level to global level. It is high time to deal with maladies of mind. It is time for every individual and human race in general to introspect for self actualisation. When it comes to self realisation or self actualisation the only promising path is resorting to meditation.

But here again I emphasise that it has to be devoid of all religious colours making it universally acceptable and adaptable too. Unless we attend to these vagaries of mind, until all its agitation is settled by meditation we can not hope for a growth in a new direction. Enough of science and technology, enough of wealth, enough of so called superfluous education. Enough of even religious sermons of all religions. Religions are thriving on a god fearing approach and none of them are truly directing us to absolute truth.

I'm neither religious nor an atheist. I believe in realising truth myself and I'm of the conviction that absolute truth or god you may call is equally intimate to every heart and soul. Let us transform ourselves that eventually transforms the world making it a better place to live in for the generations ahead.